Why Not Me?

YOUNG PEOPLE Making a Difference in the world

ALLYSON VANEK

simple truths®
Your Destination For Inspiration
an imprint of Sourcebooks, Inc.

Edited by: Alice Patenaude
Cover and internal design: VieceliDesign, Inc.

Photo Credits
Corbis: 6, 20, 18-19, 38, 44, 48-49, 86-87, 104-105
Getty: 22-23, 25, 28, 32, 42-43, 50, 54-55, 56, 60-61, 62, 66-67, 68, 70, 72-73, 76-77,
90-91, 92, 94-95, 96, 100-101,
iStockphoto: 10-11
Masterfile: 12, 24, 81, 82-83, 102
Shutterstock: 1, 7, 8, 13, 15, 20, 30-31, 33, 36-37, 39, 40, 41, 45, 51, 52, 53, 57, 58, 59, 69, 71, 74, 78, 79,
80, 90, 93, 106, 107, 108, 109, 110, 111,

Published by Simple Truths, an imprint of Sourcebooks, Inc.
P.O. Box 4410, Naperville, Illinois 60567-4410
(630) 961-3900 • Fax: (630) 961-2168
www.sourcebooks.com

Printed and bound in the United States of America

WOZ 10 9 8 7 6 5 4 3 2 1

contents

	Introduction	4
Chapter 1:	Free the Children	6
Chapter 2:	The Ladybug Foundation	12
Chapter 3:	Star Power	18
Chapter 4:	Alex's Lemonade Stand Foundation	24
Chapter 5:	Tiny Girl has a Big Heart	32
Chapter 6:	Kids Saving the Rainforest	38
Chapter 7:	Love in a Bag	44
Chapter 8:	Feeding the Hungry	50
Chapter 9:	Hoops of Hope	56
Chapter 10:	Stopping the Chain of Illiteracy	62
Chapter 11:	FUNDaFIELD: Kids helping Kids	68
Chapter 12:	The Giving Rocks Foundation	74
Chapter 13:	Little Hands Make a Big Difference	78
Chapter 14:	Helping Kids Get a Good Look at the World	84
Chapter 15:	Backpacks for New Beginnings	88
Chapter 16:	The Gift of Music	92
Chapter 17:	Sweet Tooth	96
Chapter 18:	Hats from Heaven	102
	Conclusion	106
	About the Author	110

Introduction

Recently, I had the pleasure of watching a special television segment on an amazing charity that was started by a 12-year-old-child, Craig Kielburger, who founded Free the Children in 1995. It's a story of one child's transformation from a normal, middle-class kid from the suburbs into an activist fighting against child labor on the world stage of international human rights.

During the interview, Craig was asked, **"why you?"** and his response was inspirational. He said, **"why me ... why not me?"** and declared that the future is too important to leave just to grownups. Those are very powerful words, and they started me on a journey to help the world become a better place. **That journey sparked the idea of a book about children making a difference, along with a commitment that all of the proceeds from this book will be donated to charity.** I began to ask myself the same question,

"why not me?"

While assembling the stories for this book, I was humbled by the tremendous strides my generation is making to help those among us who are most vulnerable. I am 15 years old, attending high school, playing tennis and in so many ways leading an enjoyable life. And yet, I know there is more to the journey we are all on...that one of the true purposes of life can be found in the joy of helping others. So as you read these pages, pay attention not only to the good work being performed by our generation, but also to how powerfully it has impacted those who have accepted the challenge.

I invite you to ask yourself "why not me?" and to accept the challenge to make a difference in your own way!

MY inspiration for this book began when I learned about Craig Kielburger, who was featured on *60 Minutes* twice—once when he was 12 years old, and then again eleven years later for his work in freeing children from exploitation and poverty.

Craig's journey began when he saw a newspaper article about a boy in Pakistan named Iqbal who was killed after speaking out about his plight as a slave laborer. **Iqbal was sold into slavery at the age of 4 and spent six years chained to a carpet weaving loom.** After learning of this tragedy, and without any special help from his parents, Craig decided to take action to help save other children in slavery. Since that inspired moment, the odyssey that Craig launched has touched many people's lives throughout the world.

exploitation   poverty

Like the others featured in this book, Free the Children had humble beginnings. Craig gathered some of his seventh-grade classmates to find a way to help, and help they did! Together, they wrote letters, made phone calls, and organized garage sales and lemonade stands. Craig was invited to speak to larger and larger groups and, as a 12-year-old, he took a journey to South Asia to see poverty and child labor firsthand. Craig returned home more determined than ever to crusade for children's rights.

Initially, Free the Children focused on purchasing children out of slavery so they could lead a free and full life. But **craig discovered that some of the children he had helped were falling back into the bonds of slavery.** Rather than give up, he refocused his efforts on Free the Children's "Adopt a Village" plan, a more holistic approach to breaking the bonds of slavery and poverty. This strategy addresses education, water and sanitation, health, alternative income and livelihood, and agriculture and food security in more than forty-five countries throughout the world. In 1999, Craig appeared on *Oprah*, an encounter that eventually led to Oprah Winfrey partnering with Free the Children to build schools around the world.

EMPOWERING
1.7
million YOUTH

Today, Free the Children educates, engages and empowers more than 1.7 million youth around the world with the tools, knowledge, confidence and support network they need to help change the world.

With more than 250 million child laborers pressed into work today, a tremendous amount remains to be accomplished, but Craig and the children of the world are making a difference!

"If you give kids the inspiration and the tools to change the world, they'll change their own lives in the process," said Craig. "It's a ripple effect."

"Children are likely to live up to what you believe of them."

—Lady Bird Johnson

The **Ladybug** Foundation

At just 5 years old, Hannah Taylor saw a homeless man eating out of a garbage can on a cold winter's day. It was a stark image that would not only change her life, but also that of millions of people. "I thought about that man almost every night," said Hannah. "Why, why, why?" she asked. "If everyone shared what they had, could that cure homelessness? I knew I had to do something."

By the time Hannah was 8, she had founded The Ladybug Foundation—a charity dedicated to raising money for food, shelter and the needs of homeless people.

The Ladybug Foundation name was selected because Hannah believed that homeless people needed a strong dose of good luck, which ladybugs are known to bring!

So, armed with collection jars decorated as ladybugs, the Ladybug Foundation started with bake and art sales.

Later, Hannah decided to go right to the "top" by organizing lunches with business leaders, which she calls her "Big Bosses" lunches. Those leaders, in turn, helped and encouraged Hannah. Today, the Ladybug

Foundation sponsors a National Red Scarf Day in Canada, **which helps over 50 front-line organizations,** such as soup kitchens and homeless shelters. Through Hannah's efforts, more than $2 million has been raised directly and indirectly for projects across Canada providing shelter, food and safety for homeless people. Hannah has visited many of the shelters she supports and travels throughout the world spreading her message and gathering support.

$2,000,000 **raised!**

Hannah, who is still a teenager, is certainly a big part of the good luck the Ladybug Foundation has been able to provide!

"This turned into one enormously big idea." --Hannah

who knew that an 8-year-old child
could make such a difference?

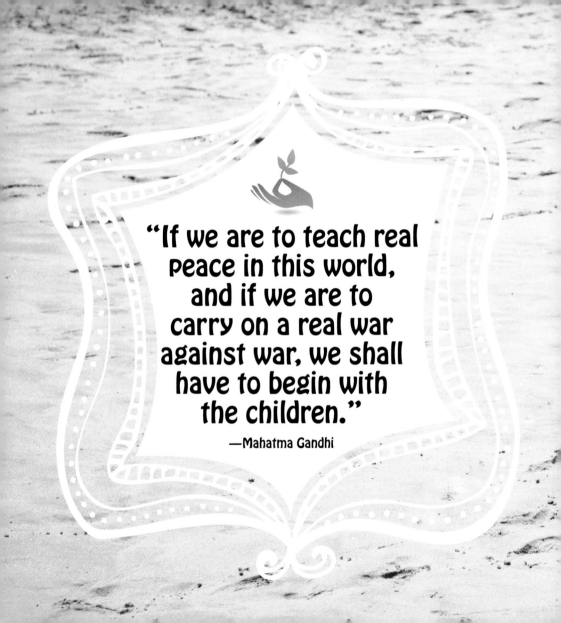

"If we are to teach real peace in this world, and if we are to carry on a real war against war, we shall have to begin with the children."

—Mahatma Gandhi

star power

Imagine going to dinner and your waiter happens to be your sports hero. Sound exciting? You bet! Now imagine a group of teenagers from Cameron County, Texas, figuring out a way to tap into that vision to benefit kids. What a great thought!

In 2007, five high school juniors decided to raise money for kids by finding sponsors to underwrite and hold a celebrity sports dinner. The main focus of their efforts was Monica's and Maggie's House—a children's advocacy center that serves child victims of abuse through prevention, intervention and treatment. Cameron County is a small poverty-stricken county on the Mexican border in South Texas, where approximately 30 percent of the kids live below the poverty line.

After approaching and gaining support of Monica's and Maggie's House, the five juniors—Julian Goza, Desi Aardema, Jared Brechot,

Cameron County, Texas

1/3

of children in
cameron county,
Texas, live below
the poverty line

Kelly Hanen and Nico Cardenas—set about securing sponsors to launch their foundation: **Teens Helping Kids.** Their mission is to raise money to fund projects through existing charities that help kids in their area.

In short order, the five were able to sign sponsors to help underwrite the first celebrity dinner, and it came off without a hitch! Dallas Cowboy Walt Garrison served as the main sports celebrity, and each of the dinner tables was served by other sports stars. At that first dinner in 2008, **Teens Helping Kids was able to raise about $58,000.**

Teens Helping Kids was presented with the Saint Joseph Academy Inaugural President's Distinguished Community Service Award. Since its inception, these students have raised nearly $400,000 to help meet the needs of children and families in their community.

COMMUNITY
SERVICE
AWARD

89%

of American households contribute to charities or religious institutions

$31,000,000,000

Warren Buffett, the investor of Berkshire Hathaway fame, became the biggest philanthropist when he donated $31 billion (initial value of the gift) to the Bill and Melinda Gates Foundation

charitable donations approached

$300B in 2011

The united states is one of only a few countries to allow tax deductions for charitable donations

In 2007, gifts from individuals made up 74.8 percent of donations at an estimated

$229 billion

At least

30,000

new charities are created each year

"Happiness...
consists in
giving, and in
serving others."

—Henry Drummond

ALEX'S LEMONADE stand Foundation

In what seems like a rite of passage, each summer, children throughout the country set up lemonade stands. A steady stream of kids and adults stop to buy a cup of lemonade and offer a few words of encouragement. The next remarkable story is about a child who was able to harness the power of that tradition.

It all began when a child, Alexandra ("Alex") Scott, who was barely 1, was diagnosed with neuroblastoma, a type of childhood cancer. By her second birthday, Alex was crawling and able to stand up with leg braces. She worked hard to gain strength and to learn how to walk. After making some progress, Alex relapsed but never lost her spirit.

Despite carrying the burden of a terrible illness at the tender age of 4, Alex looked beyond her own needs by announcing that she wanted to run a lemonade stand to help fund cancer research.

"When I get out of the hospital I want to have a lemonade stand." She said she wanted to give the money to doctors to allow them to "help other kids, like they helped me."

With those inspired words, Alex's idea became a reality and resulted in $2,000 being raised for her hospital. In the years that followed, Alex continued to both battle cancer and run lemonade stands to benefit cancer research.

Although Alex lost her battle with cancer when she was 8 years old, her vision lives on. Each year, Alex's Lemonade Stand Foundation supporters hold lemonade stands to help fund cancer research, including nearly 300 cancer studies across the country, and have resulted in over $60 million being raised. That is a lot of lemonade!

300 cancer studies ♡ funded ♡

Some of those studies were at the Children's Hospital of Philadelphia, where one of Alex's doctors, Yael Mosse, and her team studied a link between cancer and a hereditary gene mutation called anaplastic lymphoma kinase, or ALK, which seems to make certain types of cancer grow. Mosse hypothesized that crizotinib, a drug already used to successfully treat lung cancer in adults, can sometimes turn off that mutated ALK gene.

CBS News's *Sunday Morning* reported that funding from Alex's Lemonade Stand was among that used to fast-track a federally-funded crizotinib trial for nearly 80 children. The trial has shown some impressive results, including seeing the cancer disappear for some children in the study, within days or weeks.

$60 MILLION Raised

From her little lemonade stand, Alex will continue to improve children's lives for generations to come!

Alex's charity also runs some other beautiful events. Each year, they hold a **"Lemon Ball"** to thank supporters and recognize special volunteers. Part of that event includes a poetry contest designed to spread awareness of childhood cancer. Here's the winning poem written by a teenager from the 2013 contest:

Every day needs motivation
They teach the world appreciation
Despite the pain, **they smile** bright
No weaknesses, they always fight
Giving up is far from mind
Happiness blossoms inside
Thankful for the morning sun
Each sunset is a day they've won
Nothing but the **kind of heart**
Determination from the start
world, oh, world, you need to see
How children with cancer can believe
Believe in **hope** and **love** and **truth**
Embrace the honest, open youth
Believe in **goals and dreams achieved**
Believe that given beats received
It eats, attacks, breaks down their cells
But **hugs and kisses** make them well
Salt of the earth, sun of the sky
changing the world small steps at a time.

by **Megan Cullen**

29

"Children make you want to start life over."

—Muhammad Ali

Tiny Girl has a Big Heart

By **Sarah Mervosh,**
Staff Writer
The Dallas Morning News,
March 12, 2013

MCKINNEY — A Dallas man who was shot and paralyzed last year gained an unlikely ally when a third-grader set out to help him—penny by penny, prayer by prayer.

Eight-year-old Katelyn Indelicato has never met Lukas Da Cruz, described by police as an innocent bystander in a drive-by shooting in Oak Lawn. And yet, the girl has emptied her piggy bank for him and asked others for donations. So far, she's raised about $200—enough for one physical therapy session.

Katelyn doesn't wear a Disney princess costume, but she might as well. As only a child can, she lives by the black-and-white lessons of fairy tales; good conquers evil, and that's that.

"Anybody can make a difference," she said. "You can be more than what you are right now. You can do more than what you've already done."

A construction worker and amateur soccer player, Da Cruz was 21 when he was shot outside Lolita's Mexican Cuisine on Lemmon Avenue last August. Police say he was at the

wrong place at the wrong time. The shooting left him paralyzed from the waist down and in need of costly physical therapy.

Katelyn learned about Da Cruz last month through her third-grade teacher at McClure Elementary in McKinney. The teacher knows about Da Cruz through a friend of a friend.

That night, Katelyn got out her white ceramic piggy bank, the one decorated with flowers and butterflies. She uncorked it for the first time and unloaded the change into a Coinstar machine at the grocery store. Six years of loose change added up to nearly $40. **She was saving to buy an American Girl doll; instead, her money went toward physical therapy for a stranger.**

Katelyn began giving classmates knickknacks if they donated a few cents or a dollar. She made plans for a lemonade stand. On a recent weekend, Katelyn and a friend went door-to-door around her neighborhood. They handed out flyers and held out an empty peanut butter jar wrapped in pink construction paper. By Katelyn's count, they raised $144.

"Sometimes we teach our kids, and sometimes they teach us," Katelyn's mom, Shala Indelicato, said.

On a recent afternoon, Katelyn, who has blond hair and newly grown-in adult teeth, sat on the couch in her parents' McKinney home. She wiggled her feet against the coffee table as she gushed about Da Cruz.

"He's a special guy," she said of the man she's never met. "I pray every night that he can get better and one day when he's better, he can help others."

Da Cruz said he's thankful for kind strangers like Katelyn, who motivate him to stay positive. The girl's efforts are especially touching to Da Cruz's aunt and primary caretaker because she has a son who is Katelyn's age.

"I'm proud of her for caring because not everyone does," Berenice Da Cruz said. "It's what I want for my son. It's what I want for society—to care enough to do something."

In her living room, Katelyn talked on about her plans to help. Her ninth birthday is Aug. 13— three days before the anniversary of Da Cruz's shooting. She hopes to combine the dates for a big fundraiser.

"He could be able to walk again before then, though," she mused.

"You never know," her mom said, though she knows better. "Anything is possible."

"Children are
our most valuable
resource."

—Herbert Hoover,
31st U.S. president

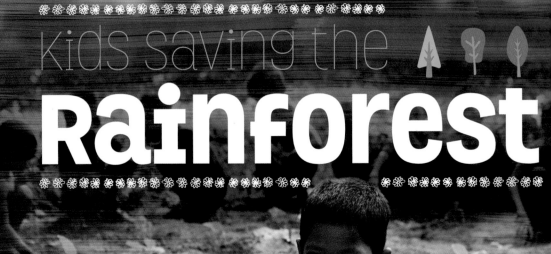

kids saving the
Rainforest

COSTA RICA is home to some of the world's most
beautiful rainforests, gorgeous coastlines and a population that is among
the most literate and friendly in the world. It was this setting that inspired
9-year-old Janine Licare and her friend, Aislin Livingstone, to found
a charity, Kids Saving the Rainforest, that helps rainforests and the
endangered animals that make those forests their home.

It all began in 1999, when **Janine and her friend painted some
rocks to sell along the road near their home in Costa Rica**
in order to earn some spending money. Sales were brisk, but after a few
days they realized that the money should be spent on something more
meaningful. They decided that "something" should be to help preserve
the rainforests.

Rainforests cover only two percent of the Earth's
total surface area but are home to 50 percent
of all plant and animal species.

2% of the Earth's total surface area is rainforests

but they are home to **50%** of all plant and animal species.

Temperate rainforests, the most valuable type, existed on almost every continent in the world, but today only 50 percent—75 million acres—of these forests remain worldwide.

A typical four-square-mile patch of rainforest in Costa Rica will contain as many as 1,500 flowering plants, 750 species of trees, 400 species of birds and 150 species of butterflies.

Now, more than ten years later, Janine's charity has blossomed. In addition to selling those rocks, Janine has founded an artisan shop and dedicated all of the proceeds to helping the rainforest. Janine has also launched a number of other initiatives to raise money, such as creating links with sister schools around the world, selling children's books and allowing donors to adopt trees, monkey bridges and patches of rainforest.

All of this tremendous energy and effort has enabled Janine to purchase patches of rainforest in Manuel Antonio, Costa Rica, establish a rehabilitation center for injured animals and run a kids' camp for both local and visiting children. Janine's story is inspiring, not only for what she has accomplished, but also because it reminds us that a child's impulse to help is not unique to a single people or country. It is shared by all the world.

"After the verb 'TO LOVE'... 'TO HELP' is the most beautiful verb in the world."

—Bertha von Suttner

Love in a Bag

Imagine being a child who is torn away from home by a foster agency, a fireman or a police officer and having to transition temporarily or permanently to a new life with little or no time to gather your belongings. At just 11 years old, the shock of the transition faced by many children caught Annie Wignall's attention, and she began searching for a way to help. Her answer was both simple and inspired: Annie wanted to create care packages for kids in crisis.

At first, Annie assembled some Care Bags for children near her home in Iowa. Then, Annie's idea blossomed and resulted in the founding of the Care Bags Foundation. Today, thanks to a small army of volunteers and contributors, **The Care Bags Foundation distributes bags to children with the help of numerous agencies who encounter kids in need throughout the world.**

Most Care Bags include basic items, such as toothbrushes, soap, dental floss, brushes and combs. Annie is also careful to include something soft, like a stuffed animal. Annie nailed it when she said,

"I know that we can't help everyone, but with your help we can make a difference, one care Bag, one child at a time."

And because Annie knows she will not meet the children who receive her Care Bags, she attaches the following poem to the outside of each:

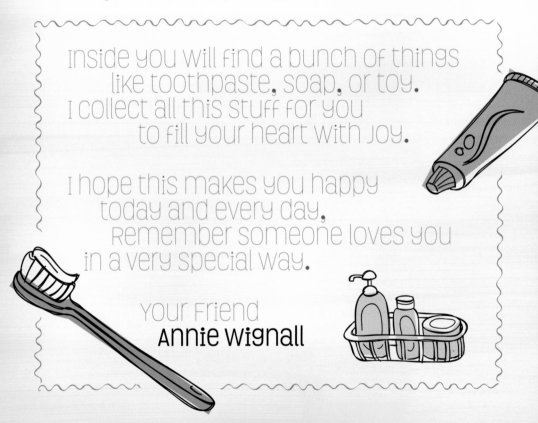

inside you will find a bunch of things
like toothpaste, soap, or toy.
I collect all this stuff for you
to fill your heart with joy.

I hope this makes you happy
today and every day,
Remember someone loves you
in a very special way.

Your Friend
Annie Wignall

Annie certainly is a friend and, as she has said, "With hand delivery by over a hundred American and international agencies, Care Bags have brought smiles, hope and tangible gifts of love to over 11,000 kids all around the world."

11,000
kids received tangible gifts

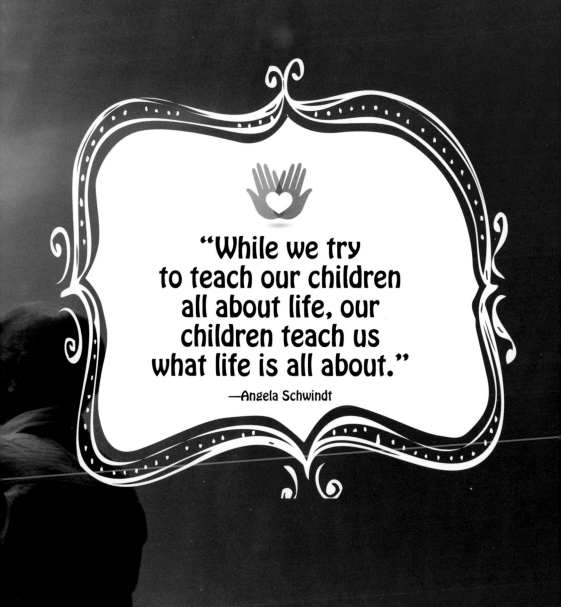

"While we try
to teach our children
all about life, our
children teach us
what life is all about."

—Angela Schwindt

Feeding the
Hungry

It's important to be persistent because success does not come easily. David Levitt's journey began when he was 11 years old, attending school in Florida. He would often visit the cafeteria and wonder what happened to all of the food left over at the end of each day. Realizing that much of the leftover food was thrown away, **David approached his school principal and asked if he could arrange to transfer the leftovers to shelters for the needy.** The principal responded with a list of reasons why David's idea was impossible, including government regulations.

While most kids would have abandoned the idea, David persisted and set about investigating those pesky government regulations. David then formulated a proposal, which he presented to the school superintendent and board. Impressed with David, they approved the plan, but the problem quickly ran into a hurdle—again those pesky government regulations!

Florida requires that food be transported in airtight containers, and with the volume of leftovers, there just was not enough money to purchase those containers. Undaunted, David personally wrote to the manufacturers of airtight containers seeking a corporate sponsor. First Brands, the owner of Glad plastic bags, agreed to send David an ongoing supply of plastic bags, and from that slow and difficult start, the idea has spread.

Today, over 100 schools
in Florida follow David's
example, resulting in over

100,000
pounds

being donated every year.

"We must teach our children to dream with their eyes open."

—Harry Edwards

HOOps

of Hope

The HIV/AIDS epidemic has caused the death of millions around the world. But the impact of the disease extends well beyond those who are ill.

When Austin Gutwein was 9 years old, he had a pen pal from Africa. As a result of that connection, he watched a video featuring the vast number of children orphaned as a result of AIDS. "I am really passionate about just helping kids, especially kids that are less fortunate than me," said Austin. He begged his parents to find a way to help, and they put him in touch with World Vision, a charity dedicated to building a better future for children.

With the help of World Vision, and turning for inspiration to a sport that he loved, Austin decided to create a "Shoot-a-Thon" to raise money for the children of AIDS victims. Austin set 2,057 free throws as his goal because that is the average number of children who

2,057
free throws shot

were orphaned due to AIDS during his school day. In 2004, Austin shot 2,057 free throws on World AIDS Day, December 1, raising almost $3,000.

Today, Hoops of Hope has grown into the largest basketball Shoot-a-Thon in the world, raising over $3 million to help orphaned children. Projects supported by Hoops of Hope include building clinics and computer labs, and providing clean water to the orphans. In this case, free throws are worth more than a single point!

$3 million
raised to help orphaned children

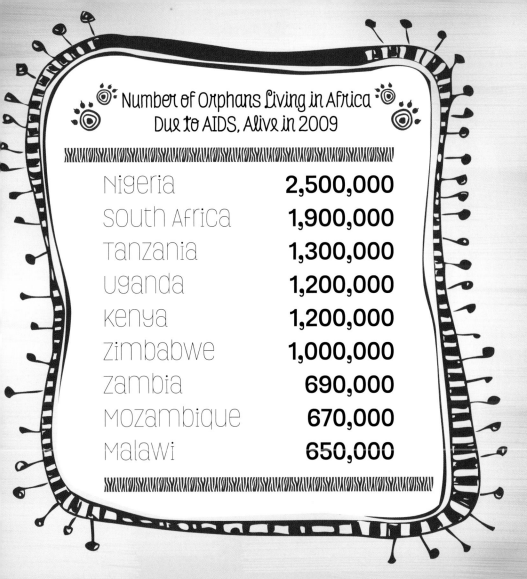

Number of Orphans Living in Africa Due to AIDS, Alive in 2009

Nigeria	2,500,000
South Africa	1,900,000
Tanzania	1,300,000
Uganda	1,200,000
Kenya	1,200,000
Zimbabwe	1,000,000
Zambia	690,000
Mozambique	670,000
Malawi	650,000

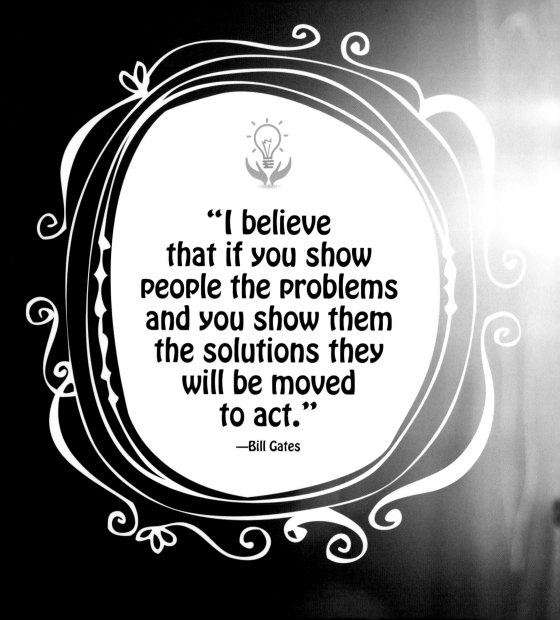

"I believe
that if you show
people the problems
and you show them
the solutions they
will be moved
to act."

—Bill Gates

stopping the chain of
illiteracy

The united states has the highest incarceration rate in the world, with more than 2.2 million inmates currently in custody. This fact is even more striking when one considers that there were less than 500,000 inmates in custody in 1990. **It is estimated that 70 percent of children whose parents have been incarcerated will wind up becoming incarcerated later in life!** These sobering statistics caught the attention of Olivia Joy Stinson when she was just 14 years old.

Each Christmas, Olivia's local church would sponsor a special celebration for the children of parents who are incarcerated. Olivia believed that these special children needed to bond together to overcome the emotional trauma of having a parent removed from their lives and founded the PEN Pals Book Club, which stands for Peers Engaged and Networking.

The PEN Pals Book Club is a literacy-focused organization that is also designed to connect and support the children of inmates. Starting with just a $500 grant from the National

2.2 MILLION INMATES IN THE US

Education Association, Olivia formed reading programs with the aid of her church in Charlotte, North Carolina, and has reached hundreds of children in her area.

"Everyone needs to be able to read because that is the key to living a productive life," Olivia says. "You need to be able to read and understand to get a decent job to be able to provide a living for your family. I think many of our youth turn to crime because they have a problem reading."

Olivia's vision is to spread her model throughout the country, stopping the chain of illiteracy for at-risk children.

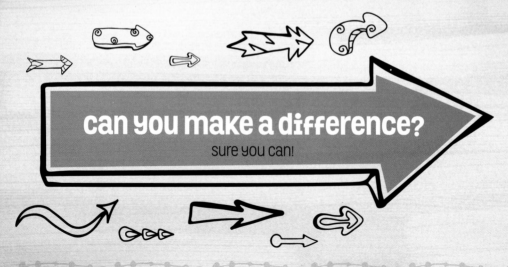

can you make a difference?

sure you can!

The United Way reports that:

$1 per week ($52 a year) supplies:
- 20 weeks of lunches for a homeless person
- 3 hours of respite care for a cancer patient
- 3 flu shots for uninsured senior citizens

$5 per week ($260 a year) buys:

- 52 home safety education kits for families with young children
- A week of groceries for 3 four-person families
- Pneumonia vaccinations for 10 senior citizens

$10 a week ($520 a year) ensures:
- 15 cases of nutritional supplements for HIV and AIDS patients
- 6 months of health education and awareness for the refugee community

- Training for 1 volunteer to work with the terminally ill

$25 a week ($1,300 a year) provides:

- 100 hours of counseling for assisted-living residents

- Psychological evaluation services for 24 special-needs children
- One week feeding and care for approximately 800 disaster victims

"No act
of kindness,
no matter
how small,
is ever
wasted."

—Aesop

FUNDaFIELD
kids helping kids

IN 2006, Garrett and Kyle Weiss had the privilege of traveling to Europe to watch some of the World Cup soccer matches, including one between Angola and Iran. During the match, the Weiss brothers spoke to the Angolan fans, who explained that kids would even use garbage bags woven into a ball to play the popular sport in their country.

After learning more about the war-torn tragic history of Angola, Garrett and Kyle decided to help. **They believed that the therapeutic power of soccer could help heal traumatized areas of the world.** To raise money, Garrett and Kyle helped organize car washes, bake sales, soccer tournaments and clubs. The results have been impressive.

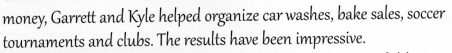

As a result of their efforts, FUNDaFIELD has built soccer fields in Uganda, Kenya and South Africa and has provided thousands of kids with the facilities and equipment needed to properly play the sport. More importantly, FUNDaFIELD has helped kids overcome tensions and mistrust that often exist in the wake of conflict. As Garrett and Kyle say,

"FUNDaFIELD can't cure disease and can't fill every empty stomach, but FUNDaFIELD can put a smile on a face, where there wasn't one before."

"If you haven't any charity in your heart, you have the worst kind of heart trouble."

—Bob Hope

The Giving ROCKS Foundation

1 in 200,000

When she was just 8 years old, Sydney Martin enjoyed collecting smooth rocks along Lake Michigan, fashioning them into necklaces she would sell to earn some money. Syd believed that she would eventually spend the money on something important, and that mission arrived just two years later when she was diagnosed with LCH, a rare blood disorder that affects only one in every 200,000 children.

Because LCH is so rare, it is **known as an "orphan" disease,** which means that there is no government funding dedicated to finding a cure. At the age of 10, Syd moved her business into high gear and has dedicated all of the proceeds to medical research for LCH. Today, Syd's prognosis is good, but she has continued designing and selling her rock necklaces both online and in retail locations to support LCH research.

"Those who bring sunshine into the lives of others cannot keep it from themselves."

—James M. Barrie

Little Hands
Make a Big Difference

Imagine being born with a congenital deformity that made one leg shorter than the other, and then facing painful surgery to correct the problem. That was the challenge that Jack O'Neill faced at the age of 6 when he entered Rush University Medical Center in Chicago, Illinois. While Jack was at the hospital, he saw the nurses throw a party for a little girl and present her with toys.

But Jack did not ask why he did not have a party or where his toys where. Instead, he committed himself to helping other children and founded "Little Hands Make a Big Difference," which is dedicated to a very simple goal. By promoting a 5K race, Little Hands raises money to buy Build-a-Bears for children in hospitals in Chicago and Rockford, Illinois. Little Hands Make a Big Difference raised more than $10,000 to brighten the days of sick children. Here is a testimonial from the family of one of the kids Jack was able to help:

Build-a-Bear

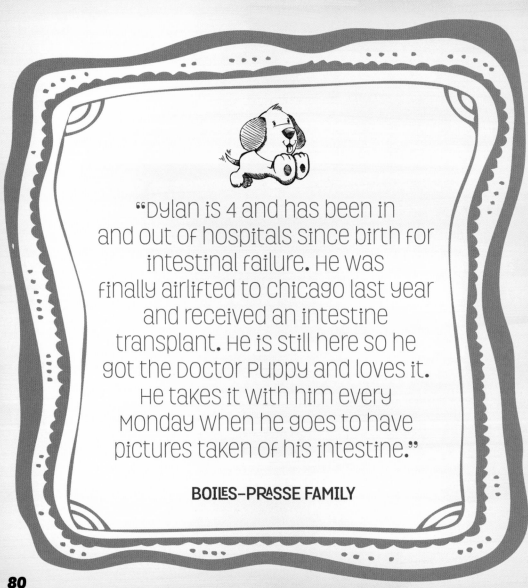

"Dylan is 4 and has been in and out of hospitals since birth for intestinal failure. He was finally airlifted to chicago last year and received an intestine transplant. He is still here so he got the Doctor Puppy and loves it. He takes it with him every Monday when he goes to have pictures taken of his intestine."

BOILES-PRASSE FAMILY

Little hands, perhaps,
but big hearts, for sure.

"How wonderful it is that nobody need wait a single moment before starting to improve the world."

—Anne Frank

Helping kids get
a GOOD LOOK
at the world

Even though Colin Byrne is only 9 years old, he likes volunteering his time for local charities, including helping out with donations for Superstorm Sandy. He takes pride in doing what he can to help others and is always there with a helping hand.

Colin's passion for **nature inspired him to begin collecting old, unused eyeglasses for delivery and distribution to third-world countries,** helping children who can't afford proper eye care so they can see the world around them and enjoy it like he does. He created flyers and wrote letters to all the classes in his school to help with his project. So far, he has collected more than 500 pairs of eyeglasses, and the project is still growing.

(Excerpted from Kidsareheroes.org)

"What does love look like?
It has the hands to help
others. It has the feet to
hasten to the poor and needy.
It has eyes to see misery and
want. It has the ears to hear
the sighs and sorrows of men.
That is what love looks like."

—Saint Augustine

Backpacks
for New Beginnings

In 2009, two brothers in the West Roxbury area of Boston noticed that backpacks were on the wish list for multiple charities, including hospitals, homeless shelters and the departments that work with foster children. Even though Tristan and Jackson Kelley were only 8 and 10 years old at the time, they decided to act.

delivered

700

backpacks filled
with school
supplies

Their initial goal was to purchase and donate 50 backpacks, so they sent a letter to friends and family asking for help, and word quickly spread. With generous donations, Tristan and Jackson were able to accomplish their goal, and more. In the summer of 2012, they managed to deliver 700 backpacks filled with school supplies to kids in need.

As Jackson said, "We wanted to give back to the kids who aren't as fortunate as we are." Tristan went on to explain, "**I like giving to the kids because it's fun, because you know you're helping out, and every time a backpack gets filled and you drop it off, you feel good.**"

In recognition of their efforts, Tristan and Jackson received an award from the Massachusetts Department of Children and Families in 2010 for helping kids who are less fortunate.

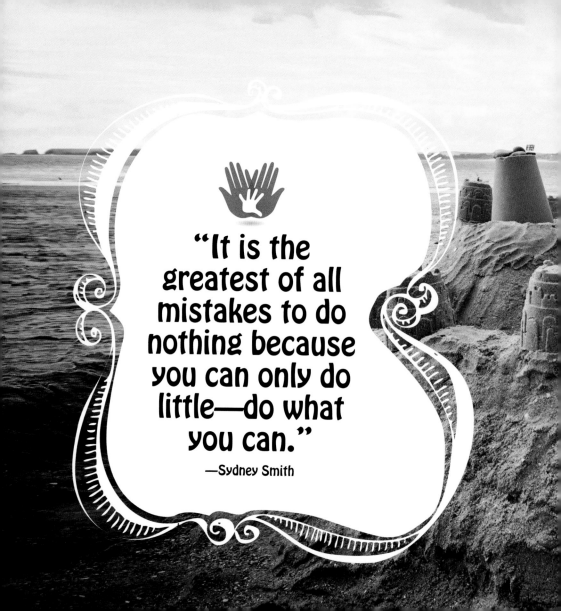

"It is the greatest of all mistakes to do nothing because you can only do little—do what you can."

—Sydney Smith

THE GiFT OF
MUSiC

There are lots of different ways to make a difference, and 10-year-old Abigail Lupi from New Jersey discovered a way to share her talents with those who need it most. It all began when Abigail performed songs for her great-grandmother's 100th birthday at an assisted-living center. The performance was so successful that Abigail thought she could bring some happiness to others if she and her friends formed a group to provide regular entertainment for the elderly.

CareGirlz was born, and today, 15 girls regularly perform for the elderly and participate in other activities to help raise money to support their efforts. A performance from CareGirlz includes Broadway songs and pop music combined with lots of dancing. As Abigail says, **"I like to brighten up people's days and help them have a fun time. If I do my best, they'll have a smile on their faces by the end."**

Abigail has been showered with awards for her efforts, including receiving the 2011 President's Volunteer Service Award and the 2010 National Golden Achievement in Service Award.

"Music in the soul can be heard by the universe."

—Lao Tzu

sweet tooth

By Christine Bockelman

(Excerpted from April 2013 *Family Circle* magazine)

At christmastime, Earlene Beko, a grandmother of seven, reflected on the meaning of the holiday for her grandchildren. "My greatest wish was for them to realize there's more joy in giving than receiving," she says.

She gathered her grandchildren around her, giving them each $50 and a challenge. **Take the $50 and make it grow by Easter**—the next time they'd all be together. Then they could donate the money to a cause of their choice.

Eight-year-old Alyssa added her own imagination to her grandmother's inspiration and ended up contributing to her community in a big way.

It wasn't until February, when she received a baking set for her birthday, that Alyssa came up with her plan. **"I decided I would earn extra money by baking cupcakes,"** she said. With the help of her mother, Debra, Alyssa made dozens of chocolate, vanilla, strawberry and lemon cupcakes. She called her business Lulu's Scrumptious Cupcakes, after her nickname. To drum up sales, she created flyers and went door-to-door in her Keizer, Oregon, neighborhood—with her mom's supervision—offering free samples.

By the time, her grandmother's deadline rolled around in April, Alyssa had raised $103, contributed $10 of her own money and added her grandmother's original $50 for a total of $163 that she planned to donate to the Boys & Girls Club. Alyssa, who is now 11, had been hanging out at the Boys & Girls Club of Salem, Marion and Polk Counties since she was 4 years old—her mom had been working there for nearly two decades—and was particularly interested in contributing to the Health and Dental Services Center, which provides free dental care to needy children.

> **"I noticed a lot of the kids wore the same clothes and that their teeth weren't really healthy," says Alyssa. "I wanted to help them."**

The club's health and dental services director, Jodi Loper, received Alyssa's gift and forwarded a copy of her note to the club's executive board members, including Chris Matheny. Chris sent the email to his wife,

Sarah, creator of a popular vegan blog and cookbook called "Peas and Thank You," suggesting they match Alyssa's $163 donation. Sarah agreed they should do something, but she wanted it to have an impact.

$5,000
DONATED

"My daughters are 5 and 7, and they love Alyssa," Sarah says. She wrote a blog post about Alyssa called **"The Hero Next Door"** and included a link to a speech that Alyssa had given at a Boys & Girls Club fundraiser a few weeks before where she emphasized that it only takes one person to make a difference.

"I wanted to prove to her—and to my girls—that those words were true." Matheny asked her blog followers to contribute to Alyssa's endeavor.

Readers of "Peas and Thank You" from all over opened their wallets, raising $2,600 in Alyssa's name. After two more contributions from club donors on Alyssa's behalf, the final amount neared $5,000. The money was used to buy more than a thousand packets of toothbrushes, toothpaste and floss.

Alyssa says she's proud of her accomplishment and has learned that helping other people makes her happy. She's even thinking about teaching a cupcake-making class at the club.

"Wherever there
is a human being,
there is an opportunity
for a kindness."

—Lucius Annaeus Seneca

Imagine undergoing chemotherapy to treat cancer and losing all of your hair. Thirteen-year-old Anthony Leanna's story began when he visited his sick grandmother and noticed that she, and many of the other patients at the hospital, had lost their hair. Anthony describes his moment:

"**My inspiration was my grandma. I spent a lot of time in hospitals when she was going through breast cancer,** and I saw a lot of the patients in hospitals without hair and asked a lot of questions. I knew that if I was in the hospital and was losing my hair, I would want a hat to wear right in the hospital. Many of the patients do not feel real well when they do get out of the hospital, and if they have a hat or two to wear when they go home, they will not have to make a special trip to a store to buy one. It was my goal to put a smile on the faces of people who were going through a very difficult time in their life."

Heavenly Hats was born! At the beginning, Anthony sent emails to companies, distributed flyers and asked businesses to display collection boxes—all for new hats. At first, Anthony struggled to get people to take him seriously, but the idea quickly took off and the response has been incredible. To date, Heavenly Hats has donated more than 1.8 million hats to medical patients in need.

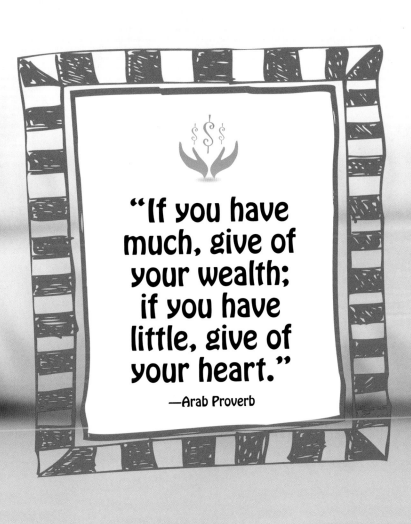

"If you have much, give of your wealth; if you have little, give of your heart."

—Arab Proverb

Conclusion

we are making a difference!

With all of the challenges people face, and the incessant drumbeat of the bad nightly news stories, it may come as a surprise to learn that the world is actually steadily becoming a better place. Consider these facts. The World Bank just released a report confirming a broad decline in extreme poverty throughout the world. The progress is so significant that the Millennium Development Goal established by the United Nations to cut extreme poverty in half before 2015 was met five years early.

In addition to reducing extreme poverty, a person's average life expectancy has grown from just 31 years in the early 20th century to

extreme poverty cut in half before 2015 was met five years early.

a worldwide average of 70 years in 2011. **violence has also been reduced.** As Harvard University cognitive neuroscientist Steven Pinker has observed, violence is far less common today than at any time in our recorded history. In fact, by almost every measure, the world is a better place. But, it is up to our generation to take our world to the next level.

average life expectancy

31 YEARS
early 20th century

70 YEARS in 2011

The progress we have seen so far is the cumulative result of millions of people dedicating their time and resources to shaping how we live, interact and grow. Each of these contributions is important not only to the people who receive the help, but also to those who take the time to give. As the great American poet Ralph Waldo Emerson observed, **"It is one of the most beautiful compensations of this life that no man can sincerely try to help another without helping himself."**

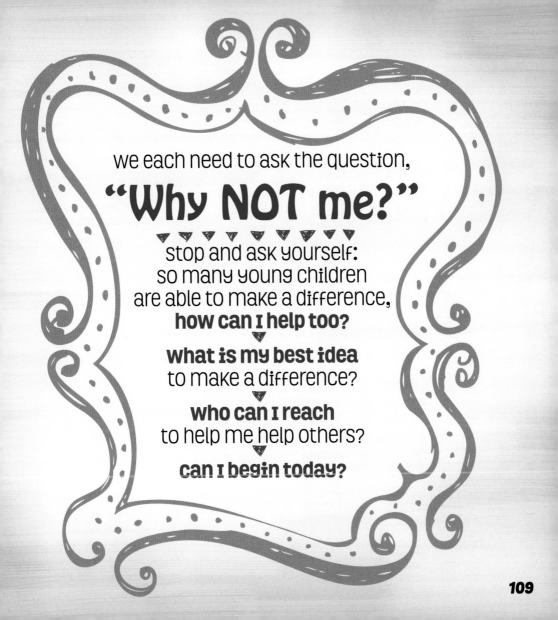

we each need to ask the question,

"Why NOT me?"

▼ ▼ ▼ ▼ ▼ ▼ ▼ ▼ ▼ ▼

stop and ask yourself:
so many young children
are able to make a difference,
how can I help too?

▼

what is my best idea
to make a difference?

▼

who can I reach
to help me help others?

▼

can I begin today?

About the Author

Allyson Vanek is 15 years old, attends high school and lives in a suburb of Chicago. She stays active playing tennis, participating in environmental club and helping a number of local charities.

Allyson is excited that her proceeds from this book have been dedicated to charity and looks forward to continuing her efforts to pursue writing as a way to make a difference.

If you have enjoyed this book we invite you to check out our entire collection of gift books, with free inspirational movies, at www.simpletruths.com. You'll discover it's a great way to inspire friends and family, or to thank your best customers and employees.

The
simple truths®
Difference